Four Furry Friends

Written by
Dorothy Willman Cummins

Illustrated by
Cheryl Proffitt

Inola, Oklahoma

Four Furry Friends

Printed in the United States of America

Written from the Heart Publishing
Inola, Oklahoma

Text by Dorothy Willman Cummins
Artwork by Cheryl Proffitt

ISBN-13: 978-0692535769

Acknowledgments

This book would not have been possible without the help of some special people.

First, thank you to my forever friend **Suzanne Young Ware**. She is the *real* Missy Young. This story is true and it is hers. She has lived a life of example to love all God's creatures.

A thank you also goes to the following:

Carol Round, inspirational writer and friend who led me through every single step of getting this book in your hands.

Cheryl Proffitt, gifted artist and friend, who brought the furry friends to life as illustrator.

Sandy Logan, Jim Elliott, Mary Ogle, Marilyn Howland and **Norma Graham**, my prayer partner friends, and my dear family members — all who encouraged and believed.

Missy Young loves all animals.

She loves her pets.

She loves the farm animals living
in her neighbors' barns and pastures.

She loves the songbirds that
sing sweetly at her birdfeeders
and in nearby trees.

She even loves the wild animals —
raccoons, foxes and deer roaming in woods
and fields around her.

She has a special love for cats.

She has several pet cats
and she also puts out food
for stray cats.

She made a special place
for stray cats
to stay on her porch.

Her porch has a roof so it has
many uses. She covered the open sides
with plastic and made a greenhouse.

The greenhouse kept her plants warm
in winter.

Missy Young wanted the cats
to be warm too, so she cut openings
in the plastic walls so the cats could
come onto the porch.

She put out pans of food and water
on the porch.

Soon her cats had company for
dinner — possums and raccoons
came too.

Missy Young just put out more food
and water.

Then she noticed that the wild cats, known as feral cats, looked cold and sad.

She decided they needed a warm place to sleep so she made beds from boxes and lined them with soft blankets.

She even put heating pads in the beds during the coldest of winter days.

On one of those cold winter days,
Missy Young looked out her window.

She saw a feral cat on her porch.
The cat was acting very strange.

Missy Young kept watching the cat.
Finally she realized that the wild cat
was giving birth.

She stood very still so she wouldn't
scare the cat, but a raccoon came
to the edge of the porch and scared
the new momma cat.

The cat ran away, leaving her
new baby alone, shivering in the cold.

Missy Young brought the tiny
orange kitten into her house.

She cleaned the kitten just
as his mother would have.
Then she tucked him into one
of the warm cat beds so his wild
mother could find him.

Late that night, the wild cat sneaked
into the box and had three more kittens.

The next morning, Missy Young
discovered the new family.

The oldest, the orange striped kitten,
was the only boy. One of his sisters
was black, another was orange,
just like him and the tiniest
of the four was orange and black
and white — a calico cat.

Missy Young loved the kittens.
She talked to them, stroked them
softly and kept them warm.

She stayed away from the porch
when their mother came to feed them
so they would get plenty to eat.

The feral mother cat was afraid
for her kittens to be near people.

She carried them in her mouth, one by one,
off into the woods and hid them.

Missy Young was afraid for the kittens.
She knew some wild animals might
hurt them.

She went to the woods and searched.

When she found the four kittens
by the creek, they were shivering
with cold.

She carried them back to the warm bed
on the porch.

She talked to the kittens. She petted them gently. They soon knew her voice and her touch and they trusted her.

The kittens knew Missy Young was their friend. Their mother did not know. She did not trust anyone.

She returned to the porch and carried her kittens into the woods.

Again, Missy Young went into the woods by the creek. She didn't see the kittens there, so she called them.

They answered with little meows until
she found their hiding spot.

She carried them back to the porch.

The kittens grew bigger and stronger.
They could walk around.

One day when Missy Young went
to retrieve the kittens, she could not
carry them all.

Scooping up the orange kitten
and his tiny sister, she told the others,
"You come on. You, too."

She walked slowly and the kittens
followed her to the porch.

By the time they were back in their beds, Missy Young had chosen a name for each kitten.

The two girl kittens that walked from the woods were You and You Too.

Their tiny sister was Little. Their big brother was named John Short because he reminded Missy Young of a school friend. Missy Young started feeding the kittens and they grew into healthy, happy cats.

They loved staying with Missy Young and refused to live in the woods with their wild mother.

The cats soon picked their favorite places.

You and You Too loved
walking in the woods.

They chose to stay outside, only coming to the porch to eat and sleep.

Little liked the warmth
of the fireplace
and decided to stay inside
during the winter.

She only went out for walks
on warm days.

John Short wanted to be a house cat.
He decided Missy Young's bed was
his bed too.

He curled up and slept on her feet,
keeping her toes and himself
warm and cozy.

He sleeps there still.

Epilogue

PARENTS AND GRANDPARENTS, as you read this book to children or with children, please consider discussing the Epilogue of Four Furry Friends with them as you consider age appropriate.

As mentioned in the Acknowledgments, Four Furry Friends is a true story. The real Missy Young provided food, shelter, veterinary care (including spay/neuter) for her furry friends.

Even the wild mother cat eventually recognized Missy Young as a friend. Years after the kittens grew into adult cats, she crawled into one of those blanket-lined boxes and went to sleep for the last time.

Just one person's acts of kindness impacted our world overpopulated with unwanted and abandoned animals. Missy Young's reward was the loving companionship of John Short, Little, You and You Too for many years. You and You Too lived to be 18 or 19. John Short and Little were with her until just months from being 22-years-old.

Message from the Author

I have always loved animals and I have always loved to write, so when my friend Susanne (the real Missy Young) introduced me to her cats and told me their story, the idea for this book came alive.

My friend and I have shared fun times since fifth grade, including getting up at daylight to ride our horses before the summer sun scorched us and rescuing ducks injured by speeding cars on the highway.

Her daddy, a veterinarian, gave me my first cat, a quirky Siamese delivered to his clinic, where he was doctored after being hit by a car and then never claimed by his owner. Susanne said, "If I had a Siamese cat, I would name him Piwacket." So I did. He lived to be 20. Then along came another Siamese cat, equally quirky. I named him Spyder and he also spent about 20 years in the family.

By then, my very favorite animals were horses and dogs, specifically basset hounds. For years I was a happy owner and backyard breeder of Palomino Quarter Horses. My daughters, Laura and Tiffany, exhibited them to youth championships. Both still love horses and dogs.

My sons, Lee and Doug, also inherited the animal lover genes. Lee and his family members are "cat people" and their pets all come from shelters. Doug prefers dogs and adopted his first shelter pet while attending college. His current canine just had her tenth birthday party!

I am grateful for the joy God's creatures have given to all of us, and I wish the same for you, my readers.

Made in the USA
Monee, IL
12 June 2023

35470175R00024